Mastering Instagram Marketing 2023

A Comprehensive Guide to Boost Your Brand's Online Presence

Alex Westwood

Copyright © 2023 by Alex Westwood

All rights reserved. No part of this publication may be reproduced, distributed, or transmitted in any form or by any means, including photocopying, recording, or other electronic or mechanical methods, without the prior written permission of the publisher, except in the case of brief quotations embodied in critical reviews and certain other noncommercial uses permitted by copyright law.

Disclaimer: The information provided in this book is for general informational purposes only. While every effort has been made to ensure the accuracy and completeness of the information, the author and publisher make no representations or warranties of any kind, express or implied, about the completeness, accuracy, reliability, suitability, or availability with respect to the book or the information, products, services, or related graphics contained in the book for any purpose. Any reliance you place on such information is therefore strictly at your own risk.

Limit of Liability/Disclaimer of Warranty: The author and publisher shall not be held liable for any damages arising from the use of this book or any information provided within. The inclusion of any links or recommendations in this book does not imply endorsement or guarantee the authenticity, accuracy, or reliability of the information contained within those links. Any reliance you place on such information is therefore strictly at your own risk.

Trademarked names, logos, and images: All names, logos, and images appearing in this book are the property of their respective owners. Their inclusion in this book does not imply any affiliation with or endorsement by the trademark holders. Any such use is purely for illustrative purposes and does not indicate any association with, or endorsement by, the trademark holders.

Acknowledgments: The author would like to express gratitude to all those who have provided support and assistance in the creation of this book, including but not limited to editors, proofreaders, designers, and mentors.

Note: The techniques and strategies discussed in this book are based on the author's experience and research. Results may vary, and success is not guaranteed. It is recommended that readers conduct their own research and consult with professionals before implementing any marketing strategies or making business decisions.

TABLE OF CONTENTS

Chapter 1 7
    Introduction to Instagram Marketing 7
Chapter 2 11
    Setting Up Your Instagram Account 11
Chapter 3 16
    Content Strategy and Planning 16
    Hashtag Strategy and Discoverability 25
Chapter 6 39
    Building an Engaged Community 39
Chapter 7 46
    Instagram Analytics and Insights 46
Chapter 8 52
    Instagram Advertising and Paid Promotions 52
Chapter 9 58
    Leveraging Instagram Shopping and E-commerce ... 58
Chapter 10 63
    Influencer Marketing on Instagram 63
Chapter 11 69
    Instagram Strategies for Different Industries 69
Chapter 12 74
    Crisis Management and Reputation Building 74
Chapter 13 78
    Future Trends in Instagram Marketing 78
Chapter 14 84

    Instagram Success Stories and Case Studies............................ 84
Chapter 15 89
    Conclusion: Your Instagram Marketing Journey Begins!........ 89
    Appendix: Helpful Resources and Tools...................................... 94

In this comprehensive guide to Instagram marketing, we will delve deep into the strategies, techniques, and tools required to succeed in leveraging the power of this popular social media platform. Whether you're a business owner, marketer, or aspiring influencer, this book will equip you with the knowledge and skills necessary to build a strong online presence, engage with your target audience, drive brand awareness, and ultimately achieve your marketing objectives. Let's embark on this exciting journey together and unlock the potential of Instagram marketing!

Chapter 1

Introduction to Instagram Marketing

1.1 The Power of Instagram in the Digital Age

In today's digital age, social media platforms play a vital role in connecting people, fostering communities, and driving business growth.

Among these platforms, Instagram has emerged as a powerhouse, boasting over a billion monthly active users. With its visually appealing nature and highly engaged user base, Instagram has become a go-to platform for businesses and individuals to showcase their products, services, and personal brands.

Instagram's power lies in its ability to captivate and inspire through stunning visual content. It allows users to share photos, videos, stories, and more, providing a rich and immersive experience.

The platform has transcended its initial purpose as a photo-sharing app and has evolved into a robust marketing tool that enables businesses to reach a global audience and build meaningful connections.

1.2 Understanding Instagram's Features and User Demographics

To harness the power of Instagram, it's crucial to understand its features and the demographics of its user base. Instagram offers various features designed to enhance user experience and facilitate engagement. These include the main feed, Instagram Stories, IGTV, Reels, Shopping, and more. Each feature presents unique opportunities for marketers to create compelling content, drive engagement, and connect with their target audience.

Furthermore, understanding Instagram's user demographics is essential for effective targeting. Instagram attracts a diverse user base, but it tends to be particularly popular among younger audiences. According to recent statistics, a significant percentage of Instagram users are aged between 18 and 34. However, the platform's reach extends beyond this demographic, making it a valuable marketing channel for a wide range of businesses and industries.

1.3 Benefits of Instagram Marketing for Businesses

Instagram marketing offers numerous benefits for businesses of all sizes. Here are some key advantages:

1.3.1 Increased Brand Awareness: Instagram provides a platform for businesses to showcase their brand identity, values, and unique offerings. By consistently sharing high-quality and visually appealing content, businesses can raise brand awareness and establish a recognizable presence in the minds of their target audience.

1.3.2 Enhanced Engagement: Instagram's highly visual nature fosters engagement and interaction. With features like likes, comments, direct messages, and story replies, businesses can directly connect with their audience, build relationships, and receive valuable feedback.

1.3.3 Expanded Reach and Global Exposure: Instagram's vast user base and global reach allow businesses to expand their reach beyond geographical boundaries. With the right strategies, businesses can tap into new markets, attract international customers, and establish a global brand presence.

1.3.4 Access to Targeted Audiences: Instagram provides powerful targeting options to ensure your content reaches the right audience. Through various parameters like demographics, interests, and behaviors, businesses can effectively target their ideal customers and increase the chances of converting them into loyal followers and customers.

1.3.5 Sales and Conversion Opportunities: Instagram's shopping features, such as product tags and shoppable posts, enable businesses to showcase their products or services directly to their audience and drive sales. With a seamless shopping experience, businesses can turn engaged followers into paying customers.

1.3.6 Influencer Collaborations: Instagram is a hub for influencers who have built substantial followings and credibility within their niches. Partnering with relevant influencers can amplify a business's reach, improve brand perception, and drive conversions through authentic recommendations and endorsements.

As we progress through this book, we will explore various strategies, techniques, and best practices that will empower you to leverage Instagram's power for your marketing endeavors. From optimizing your profile to crafting compelling content and implementing advanced marketing tactics, you will gain the knowledge and skills needed to succeed in the dynamic world of Instagram marketing.

Chapter 2

Setting Up Your Instagram Account

2.1 Creating a Business Account

In today's digital landscape, having a dedicated business account on Instagram is crucial for effective marketing. Creating a business account provides access to essential features and analytics that can help you understand your audience, track your performance, and make informed marketing decisions. Here are the steps to create a business account on Instagram:

Step 1: Download the Instagram App: Start by downloading the Instagram app from the App Store or Google Play Store. Alternatively, you can visit the Instagram website on your desktop.

Step 2: Sign Up for an Account: Open the app and click on "Sign Up" to create a new account. You can choose to sign up with either your email address or phone number.

Step 3: Choose a Username: Select a unique username that represents your business. Ideally, it should be aligned with your brand and easy to remember.

Step 4: Complete Your Profile Information: Fill in your profile information, including your business name, website, and bio. This information will help users learn more about your brand and navigate to your website.

Step 5: Connect Your Facebook Page (Optional): If you have a Facebook Page for your business, you can link it to your Instagram account. This allows for seamless cross-posting and access to additional features such as Instagram Shopping.

Step 6: Switch to a Business Account: Once your account is set up, navigate to your profile, click on the menu icon (three horizontal lines), and go to "Settings." From there, select "Account" and then "Switch to Professional Account." Follow the prompts to set up a business account.

2.2 Optimizing Your Profile for Maximum Impact

Your Instagram profile is often the first impression users have of your business. It's essential to optimize it to make a strong impact and encourage users to engage with your content. Here are some key elements to consider when optimizing your profile:

2.2.1 Profile Picture: Choose a high-resolution profile picture that clearly represents your brand. It can be your company logo, a professional headshot, or a recognizable brand symbol. Ensure it is visually appealing and easily identifiable even at a small size.

2.2.2 Username: Your username should be consistent with your brand and easy to remember. If possible, use your business name or a shortened version of it. Avoid using numbers or symbols that may make it difficult for users to find you.

2.2.3 Bio: Craft a compelling and concise bio that conveys your brand's value proposition and personality. Use relevant keywords and hashtags to improve discoverability. You can also include a call-to-action (CTA) to encourage users to take specific actions, such as visiting your website or signing up for your newsletter.

2.2.4 Website Link: Utilize the link in your bio to drive traffic to your website or a specific landing page. Consider using tools like Linktree or a custom landing page to provide multiple links if needed.

2.2.5 Highlights: Instagram Highlights allow you to curate and showcase your best Stories. Create highlights that reflect different aspects of your business, such as products, services, behind-the-scenes, testimonials, or events. Use eye-catching cover images and organize your highlights strategically to provide a visually appealing and informative experience for visitors.

2.2.6 Category: Instagram provides a category selection feature for business accounts. Choose the most relevant category that accurately represents your business to enhance discoverability in search and explore functionalities.

2.2.7 Contact Information: Make it easy for users to get in touch with you by providing contact information. Include your email address, phone number, or a contact button linked to a contact form.

2.3 Crafting an Effective Bio and Profile Picture

Your Instagram bio and profile picture are crucial elements that can make or break a user's decision to follow your account. Here are some tips for crafting an effective bio and selecting an impactful profile picture:

2.3.1 Bio Tips:
- Keep it concise: Instagram bios have limited character space, so make every word count. Focus on conveying your unique value proposition and what sets your brand apart.
- Use keywords and hashtags: Incorporate relevant keywords and hashtags related to your industry, niche, or target audience. This improves your discoverability in search and explore functionalities.
- Inject personality: Let your brand's personality shine through your bio. Use a tone that aligns with your brand voice and resonates with your target audience.
- Include a CTA: Encourage users to take action by including a clear call-to-action in your bio. Whether it's visiting your website, subscribing to your newsletter, or checking out your latest product, a CTA helps drive user engagement.

2.3.2 Profile Picture Tips:

- Choose a high-quality image: Your profile picture represents your brand, so ensure it is of high resolution and reflects the professionalism and quality associated with your business.
- Stay consistent: Use the same profile picture across all your social media platforms to maintain a cohesive brand identity and make it easier for users to recognize your brand.
- Ensure visibility at small sizes: Keep in mind that your profile picture will appear as a small thumbnail in comments and search results. Select an image that is easily recognizable even at a reduced size.

By creating a business account and optimizing your profile effectively, you establish a strong foundation for your Instagram marketing efforts. A well-crafted bio and a visually appealing profile picture help attract your target audience, convey your brand's personality, and encourage users to engage with your content.

Chapter 3

Content Strategy and Planning

In the realm of Instagram marketing, content is king. A well-defined content strategy sets the foundation for a successful Instagram presence. In this chapter, we will explore the key aspects of content strategy and planning to help you engage your audience and achieve your marketing goals.

3.1 Defining Your Brand Identity and Voice

Before diving into content creation, it's crucial to define your brand identity and voice. Your brand identity encompasses your values, mission, and unique selling proposition. It forms the core of your content and guides your messaging across Instagram.

Consider the following when defining your brand identity and voice:

- Core Values: Identify the values that drive your brand. What do you stand for? How do these values align with your target audience's values?

- Tone and Personality: Determine the tone and personality you want to project. Are you playful and lighthearted, or serious and professional? Your tone should resonate with your target audience.

- Visual Style: Define your brand's visual style, including colors, fonts, and aesthetics. Consistency in visual elements helps create a cohesive and recognizable brand presence.

- Storytelling: Craft a compelling brand story that communicates your brand's journey, values, and impact. Storytelling humanizes your brand and connects with your audience on an emotional level.

By establishing a clear brand identity and voice, you can create content that is authentic, relatable, and consistent with your brand's essence.

3.2 Identifying Your Target Audience

Understanding your target audience is vital for tailoring your content to their preferences and interests. By identifying your target audience, you can create content that resonates with them and builds meaningful connections. Consider the following steps when identifying your target audience:

- Demographics: Determine the age, gender, location, and other relevant demographics of your target audience. This information helps shape your content and messaging.

- Psychographics: Dive deeper into your audience's interests, values, motivations, and behaviors. What are their pain points, aspirations, and challenges? This insight allows you to create content that addresses their specific needs.

- Competitor Analysis: Study your competitors' audiences to identify overlaps and unique opportunities. Analyze their followers, engagement patterns, and content strategies to gain insights.

- Customer Surveys and Feedback: Conduct surveys or seek feedback from your existing customers to understand their preferences, interests, and expectations. This firsthand information is invaluable for crafting targeted content.

By understanding your target audience, you can create content that resonates with their needs, interests, and aspirations, increasing engagement and driving meaningful interactions.

3.3 Planning Engaging and Relevant Content

To maximize the impact of your Instagram marketing efforts, strategic content planning is essential. Here are key steps to planning engaging and relevant content:

- Content Pillars: Define core content pillars that align with your brand identity, target audience, and business objectives. These pillars represent the key themes and topics you will focus on in your content strategy.

- Content Formats: Determine the types of content you will create, such as photos, videos, carousels, quotes, behind-the-scenes glimpses, tutorials, or user-generated content (UGC). Variety in content formats keeps your feed visually appealing and engaging.

- Content Calendar: Develop a content calendar to organize your posting schedule and ensure consistency. Plan your content in advance, including captions, visuals, and relevant hashtags. Consider incorporating timely events, holidays, or industry-specific occasions.

- Visual Cohesion: Maintain a consistent visual style by using a specific color palette, filters, and editing techniques. This cohesion creates a visually appealing and recognizable brand aesthetic.

- Mix of Content: Strike a balance between promotional and non-promotional content. While promoting your products or services is important, prioritize value-driven content that educates, inspires, entertains, or solves problems for your audience.

- Engaging Captions: Craft compelling captions that resonate with your audience. Use storytelling, ask questions, spark discussions, or encourage user participation to drive engagement and build relationships.

By planning your content strategically, you can maintain consistency, ensure a cohesive visual aesthetic, and provide valuable content that keeps your audience engaged and interested in your brand.

3.4 Utilizing User-Generated Content (UGC)

User-genercted content (UGC) is a powerful tool in your Instagram content strategy. UGC refers to content created by your audience or customers that features or mentions your brand.

Leveraging UGC offers several benefits:

- Authenticity: UGC provides social proof and authenticity, as it showcases real experiences and opinions of your customers. This builds trust and credibility among your audience.

- Engagement and Community Building: By featuring UGC, you foster a sense of community and encourage your audience to participate. This creates a deeper connection with your brand and motivates others to contribute their own content.

- Diverse Perspectives: UGC brings in diverse perspectives, showcasing different use cases, creative interpretations, and personal stories related to your brand. This enriches your content and broadens its appeal.

To encourage UGC, consider the following strategies:

- Create branded hashtags and encourage your audience to use them when sharing content related to your brand.

- Run contests, challenges, or giveaways that encourage your audience to create and share content using your products or services.

- Regularly engage with your audience's content by liking, commenting, and sharing it on your own Instagram account. This encourages further participation.

By incorporating UGC into your content strategy, you tap into the power of user-generated content, strengthen your brand community, and foster deeper connections with your audience.

3.5 Leveraging Instagram Stories, Reels, and IGTV

Instagram offers various features beyond the main feed, including Instagram Stories, Reels, and IGTV. Leveraging these features can significantly enhance your content strategy and engagement levels. Let's explore how to utilize each of these features effectively:

3.5.1 Instagram Stories:

- Behind-the-Scenes: Showcase the human side of your brand by sharing behind-the-scenes moments, team activities, or product creation processes. This builds authenticity and strengthens the connection with your audience.

- Product Teasers and Launches: Generate excitement around upcoming products or services by sharing teasers, sneak peeks, or countdowns on your Stories. This creates anticipation and encourages your audience to stay engaged.

- Interactive Features: Utilize interactive stickers, polls, quizzes, or question boxes to engage your audience and gather valuable insights. Encourage users to participate and share their opinions or experiences.

- Story Highlights: Organize your Stories into Highlights that remain visible on your profile. Use highlights to showcase different aspects of your brand, products, or events. This helps new visitors quickly understand your brand and access relevant information.

3.5.2 Reels:

- Short-Form Videos: Create engaging and entertaining short videos using Reels. Experiment with trends, challenges, tutorials, or share valuable tips related to your industry or niche.

Capitalize on the creative potential of Reels to capture attention and expand your reach.

- Explore Page Opportunities: Reels have significant visibility on the Explore page, making it an excellent opportunity to attract new followers and increase brand exposure. Focus on creating compelling Reels that resonate with your target audience.

3.5.3 IGTV:

- Long-Form Content: IGTV allows you to share longer videos, making it ideal for in-depth tutorials, interviews, product demonstrations, or educational content. Develop a content strategy for IGTV that complements your overall brand message and provides value to your audience.

- Series and Episodes: Consider creating episodic content or series on IGTV to keep your audience engaged and coming back for more. This format works well for storytelling, educational series, or behind-the-scenes glimpses.

- Cross-Promotion: Promote your IGTV videos on your Instagram feed and Stories to maximize their visibility and reach. Tease the content, highlight key takeaways, or provide a sneak peek to generate interest.

By leveraging Instagram Stories, Reels, and IGTV, you expand your content repertoire and tap into different formats that cater to varying audience preferences.

These features provide unique opportunities for engagement, discoverability, and storytelling.

In Chapter 3, we explored the importance of content strategy and planning on Instagram. By defining your brand identity and voice, identifying your target audience, planning engaging content, utilizing user-generated content, and leveraging Instagram's features effectively, you can create a compelling and impactful Instagram presence that resonates with your audience and achieves your marketing goals.

Chapter 4

Hashtag Strategy and Discoverability

In the vast landscape of Instagram, hashtags play a crucial role in boosting discoverability, increasing reach, and connecting with your target audience. This chapter delves into the importance of hashtags in Instagram marketing and provides strategies for researching and utilizing relevant hashtags, developing branded hashtags, and engaging with hashtag communities effectively.

4.1 The Importance of Hashtags in Instagram Marketing

Hashtags are words or phrases preceded by the pound symbol (#) used to categorize and organize content on Instagram. They serve as powerful tools for increasing your content's visibility, reaching a wider audience, and driving engagement. Here's why hashtags are vital in your Instagram marketing efforts:

4.1.1 Increased Discoverability: Hashtags make your content discoverable beyond your immediate followers. When users search or click on a hashtag, they are taken to a feed that includes all posts containing that hashtag. By using relevant hashtags, you increase the chances of your content appearing in these feeds, attracting new users to your account.

4.1.2 Targeted Reach: Hashtags allow you to target specific niches, industries, or interests. By using relevant and specific hashtags, you can ensure your content reaches the right audience—those who are interested in and actively searching for content related to your industry or niche.

4.1.3 Trending Topics and Virality: Hashtags are often used to participate in trending conversations, events, or challenges. By jumping on relevant trends and incorporating popular hashtags, you increase your chances of your content going viral, attracting significant attention, and gaining new followers.

4.1.4 Community Engagement: Hashtags foster community engagement by connecting like-minded individuals around a specific topic or interest. Engaging with hashtag communities can help you build relationships, gain followers, and establish your authority within your industry or niche.

Now that we understand the importance of hashtags, let's explore strategies for researching and utilizing relevant hashtags effectively.

4.2 Researching and Utilizing Relevant Hashtags

To maximize the impact of hashtags on your Instagram marketing, it's crucial to research and use relevant hashtags that align with your content, target audience, and marketing goals. Here's a step-by-step process for researching and utilizing hashtags:

4.2.1 Identify Relevant Keywords: Start by identifying keywords related to your industry, niche, or specific content. These keywords should reflect what your target audience would search for when looking for content like yours.

4.2.2 Hashtag Research Tools: Utilize hashtag research tools like Hashtagify, RiteTag, or Instagram's own search functionality to find relevant and popular hashtags. These tools provide insights into hashtag popularity, related hashtags, and hashtag performance metrics.

4.2.3 Mix of Popular and Niche Hashtags: Strike a balance between popular and niche hashtags. Popular hashtags have high competition, but they also attract a larger audience. Niche hashtags have a more targeted audience, allowing you to connect with a specific group of users who are highly interested in your content.

4.2.4 Hashtag Size and Competition: Consider the size and competition of hashtags. Using smaller, more specific hashtags with less competition gives you a higher chance of being seen in the hashtag feed and reaching engaged users.

4.2.5 Hashtag Relevance: Ensure the hashtags you use are relevant to your content. Irrelevant or spammy hashtags can harm your reputation and attract the wrong audience. Choose hashtags that accurately represent the content and align with your brand values.

4.2.6 Create Hashtag Lists: Develop a collection of hashtag lists tailored to different content themes, products, or campaigns. This allows you to easily access and use relevant hashtags when planning and posting content.

4.2.7 Evolving Hashtag Strategy: Continuously monitor the performance of your hashtags and make adjustments as needed. Analyze which hashtags drive the most engagement, reach, and followers. Experiment with new hashtags and retire ones that are not performing well.

By researching and utilizing relevant hashtags, you increase your content's discoverability, target the right audience, and improve engagement levels. Next, let's explore how you can develop your own branded hashtags.

4.3 Developing Your Branded Hashtags

Branded hashtags are unique to your brand and help create a distinct online identity. They enable you to foster community engagement, encourage user-generated content, and strengthen brand awareness. Here are steps to develop your branded hashtags:

4.3.1 Reflect Your Brand: Create a hashtag that reflects your brand identity, values, or tagline. It should be memorable, easy to spell, and align with your brand messaging.

4.3.2 Keep it Short and Simple: Branded hashtags should be concise and easy to remember. Long and complicated hashtags are less likely to be used consistently by your audience.

4.3.3 Promote Consistently: Consistently promote your branded hashtags across your Instagram account, website, marketing materials, and other social media platforms. Encourage your audience to use your branded hashtags when sharing content related to your brand.

4.3.4 Hashtags for Campaigns and Contests: Create specific branded hashtags for campaigns, contests, or special events. This allows you to track and gather user-generated content associated with these initiatives.

4.3.5 Engage with Branded Hashtag Users: Monitor and engage with users who use your branded hashtags. Like, comment, or share their content to encourage further participation and build a sense of community around your brand.

By developing branded hashtags, you create a unique identifier for your brand, encourage user participation, and enhance brand recognition and loyalty.

4.4 Engaging with Hashtag Communities

Engaging with hashtag communities is a valuable strategy to build relationships, increase visibility, and establish your brand's authority within your industry or niche. Here's how to effectively engage with hashtag communities:

4.4.1 Discover Relevant Hashtag Communities: Identify relevant hashtags that have active and engaged communities. Explore the content, engagement levels, and conversations surrounding these hashtags to understand the dynamics and opportunities for engagement.

4.4.2 Participate and Contribute: Engage with posts and discussions within the hashtag communities by liking, commenting, and sharing valuable insights. Be genuine, add value to the conversation, and avoid being overly promotional.

4.4.3 Follow Hashtag Contributors: Follow users who consistently contribute high-quality content within the hashtag communities. This allows you to stay connected with their content, engage with them regularly, and potentially build collaborative relationships.

4.4.4 Collaborate and Co-create: Collaborate with other users within the hashtag communities to create content, cross-promote each other, or participate in joint initiatives. This expands your reach, introduces you to new audiences, and strengthens your position within the community.

4.4.5 Create a Community Hashtag: Consider creating a community hashtag specific to your industry or niche. Encourage others to use this hashtag when sharing content related to the community. Engage with users who utilize the community hashtag to foster a sense of belonging and collective identity.

Engaging with hashtag communities allows you to tap into existing conversations, build relationships, and establish yourself as an active and valuable participant within your industry or niche.

In Chapter 4, we explored the significance of hashtags in Instagram marketing. By researching and utilizing relevant hashtags, developing your branded hashtags, and engaging with hashtag communities, you enhance discoverability, expand your reach, and foster connections with your target audience. Implementing an effective hashtag strategy is essential for optimizing your Instagram marketing efforts.

Chapter 5

Captivating Visuals and Photography Tips

In the visually-driven world of Instagram, captivating visuals play a vital role in attracting and engaging your audience. This chapter focuses on the importance of high-quality visuals, composition and lighting techniques for stunning photos, utilizing editing apps and filters, and incorporating videos and GIFs for increased engagement. Let's dive in!

5.1 Importance of High-Quality Visuals on Instagram

On Instagram, where users are constantly scrolling through their feeds, high-quality visuals are essential for grabbing attention and making a lasting impression. Here's why they matter:

5.1.1 First Impressions: With thousands of posts competing for attention, a high-quality visual is your chance to make a strong first impression. It entices users to pause, explore, and engage with your content.

5.1.2 Brand Perception: High-quality visuals reflect the professionalism and quality of your brand. They convey a sense of credibility and trustworthiness, encouraging users to perceive your brand positively.

5.1.3 Storytelling: Compelling visuals have the power to tell stories, evoke emotions, and convey your brand's message effectively. They can capture attention, spark curiosity, and generate interest in your content.

5.1.4 Stand Out from the Crowd: In a saturated Instagram environment, high-quality visuals help your posts stand out. They make your content more memorable, increasing the likelihood of users engaging with and sharing your posts.

Now that we understand the importance of high-quality visuals, let's explore some composition and lighting techniques to capture stunning photos.

5.2 Composition and Lighting Techniques for Stunning Photos

Composition and lighting are key elements in photography that can significantly enhance the impact of your visuals. Here are some techniques to consider:

5.2.1 Rule of Thirds: The rule of thirds is a fundamental principle of composition. Imagine breaking your frame into a 3x3 grid, and place the main elements of your photo along these gridlines or at their intersections. This creates a balanced and visually appealing composition.

5.2.2 Leading Lines: Incorporate leading lines, such as roads, pathways, or architectural lines, to draw the viewer's eye into the photo and create a sense of depth and dimension.

5.2.3 Framing: Use natural elements or architectural structures to frame your subject. This adds context, creates visual interest, and directs the viewer's attention to the focal point.

5.2.4 Symmetry and Patterns: Symmetry and patterns can create visually striking compositions. Look for symmetry in architecture, nature, or everyday objects to add balance and aesthetic appeal to your photos.

5.2.5 Negative Space: Embrace negative space, the empty areas in your composition, to create a sense of minimalism and focus on the main subject. This allows the viewer to appreciate the subject's details and adds a sense of elegance to the photo.

5.2.6 Golden Hour: Take advantage of the golden hour, the period shortly after sunrise or before sunset when the lighting s soft and warm. This natural lighting creates a magical ambiance, enhances colors, and adds depth and dimension to your photos.

5.2.7 Backlighting: Experiment with backlighting by positioning your subject in front of a light source. This creates a beautiful halo effect and can add drama and mood to your photos.

By implementing these composition and lighting techniques, you can elevate the visual impact of your photos, making them more captivating and engaging to your audience.

5.3 Using Editing Apps and Filters

Editing plays a crucial role in enhancing your visuals and maintaining a consistent aesthetic on Instagram. Here are some tips for using editing apps and filters effectively:

5.3.1 Choose the Right Editing App: There are numerous photo editing apps available, each with its unique features and capabilities. Experiment with different apps such as Adobe Lightroom, VSCO, or Snapseed to find the one that suits your editing style and needs.

5.3.2 Adjust Exposure and Contrast: Use editing tools to adjust the exposure and contrast of your photos. This helps in achieving a balanced and well-lit image.

5.3.3 Enhance Colors: Enhance the colors in your photos by adjusting saturation, vibrance, and individual color channels. Be mindful of maintaining a natural and realistic look.

5.3.4 Sharpen and Reduce Noise: Use the sharpening tool to enhance the details and clarity of your photos.

Additionally, reduce noise to minimize graininess in low-light or high ISO images.

5.3.5 Consistency in Editing: Establish a consistent editing style or preset for your photos. This helps create a cohesive visual identity for your brand and ensures a unified look across your Instagram feed.

5.3.6 Use Filters Wisely: Filters can be a quick way to enhance your photos, but use them sparingly and purposefully. Avoid overusing filters that drastically alter the colors or overall look of your images. Strive for a balanced and natural aesthetic.

Remember, editing should enhance your visuals, not completely transform them. Maintain the authenticity and integrity of your images while adding a touch of creativity and style.

5.4 Incorporating Videos and GIFs for Increased Engagement

In addition to static images, incorporating videos and GIFs into your Instagram content can significantly boost engagement and capture your audience's attention. Here's how to leverage these dynamic elements effectively

5.4.1 Video Content: Experiment with different types of video content, such as tutorials, behind-the-scenes footage, product demonstrations, or storytelling videos.

Keep them concise, engaging, and aligned with your brand's messaging.

5.4.2 Instagram Reels: Utilize Instagram Reels, a short-form video format, to create entertaining and informative content. Leverage the Reels features like text overlays, effects, and music to make your videos more engaging and shareable.

5.4.3 GIFs and Boomerangs: Incorporate GIFs and Boomerangs, which are short looping videos, into your content strategy. These playful and eye-catching elements can add a touch of fun and excitement to your posts.

5.4.4 Story Highlights: Use Instagram's Story Highlights feature to curate and showcase your best video content. Organize them into themed categories that align with your brand or products for easy access and extended engagement.

Videos and GIFs offer a dynamic and interactive way to connect with your audience. By incorporating them into your content strategy, you can diversify your visual content and increase engagement levels.

In Chapter 5, we explored the significance of captivating visuals and photography tips on Instagram. By prioritizing high-quality visuals, mastering composition and lighting techniques, using editing apps and filters effectively, and incorporating videos and GIFs, you can create visually stunning and engaging content that resonates with your audience. Remember, visual storytelling is a powerful tool on Instagram, and investing time and effort into creating captivating visuals will pay off in terms of increased engagement and brand recognition.

Chapter 6

Building an Engaged Community

In the world of Instagram marketing, building an engaged community is crucial for the success of your brand. This chapter focuses on strategies to encourage user engagement and interaction, responding to comments and direct messages, hosting contests, giveaways, and challenges, as well as collaborating with influencers and partners. Let's explore these key components of community building.

6.1 Encouraging User Engagement and Interaction

User engagement and interaction are the lifeblood of a thriving Instagram community. Here are some strategies to encourage active participation from your followers:

6.1.1 Compelling Captions: Craft compelling captions that prompt your audience to engage. Ask questions, seek their opinions, or encourage them to tag a friend who would resonate with the content. This invites conversation and creates a sense of connection.

6.1.2 Call-to-Action (CTA): Include a clear call-to-action in your captions or posts. Whether it's asking users to like, comment, share, or save the post, a CTA encourages immediate action and boosts engagement.

6.1.3 Respond Promptly: Actively monitor and respond to comments and direct messages from your audience. Show genuine interest in their thoughts, answer their questions, and engage in meaningful conversations. This fosters a sense of community and makes your followers feel valued.

6.1.4 Encourage User-Generated Content (UGC): Prompt your followers to create and share content related to your brand. Encourage them to use a specific hashtag or tag your brand in their posts. UGC not only generates buzz but also serves as social proof, showcasing the positive experiences and engagement of your community.

6.1.5 Polls and Surveys: Utilize Instagram's interactive features such as polls and surveys in your Stories to gather feedback and opinions from your audience. This not only encourages participation but also provides valuable insights for your brand.

6.1.6 Live Q&A Sessions: Host live Q&A sessions on Instagram Live or through the Questions sticker in your Stories. This allows your followers to directly engage with you, ask questions, and receive real-time responses. It builds a sense of authenticity and fosters a deeper connection with your community.

By implementing these strategies, you create an environment that encourages active participation, conversation, and connection among your audience members.

6.2 Responding to Comments and Direct Messages

Engaging with your audience goes beyond just encouraging them to participate. Responding to comments and direct messages is essential for building relationships and fostering a strong community. Here's how to effectively manage these interactions:

6.2.1 Timely Responses: Aim to respond to comments and direct messages promptly. This shows your followers that you value their input and are actively engaged in the community. Set aside dedicated time to engage with your audience and address their inquiries or feedback.

6.2.2 Personalized Messages: When responding to direct messages, personalize your replies. Use the person's name and refer to their specific query or comment. This demonstrates your attentiveness and helps build a genuine connection with your audience.

6.2.3 Positive and Constructive Tone: Maintain a positive and constructive tone in your responses. Even if faced with negative comments or feedback, respond professionally and seek to address concerns or provide solutions. Avoid engaging in arguments or public disputes, as this can harm your brand's reputation.

6.2.4 Tag and Mention Users: When appropriate, tag or mention users in your responses. This not only notifies them of your reply but also gives them visibility within your community. It shows that you value their contribution and fosters a sense of belonging.

6.2.5 Set Clear Boundaries: While it's important to engage with your audience, it's equally important to set clear boundaries. Define guidelines for acceptable behavior and establish rules for engagement. This helps maintain a positive and respectful community environment.

By actively responding to comments and direct messages, you demonstrate your commitment to building relationships and fostering a sense of community, leading to increased loyalty and engagement.

6.3 Hosting Contests, Giveaways, and Challenges

Contests, giveaways, and challenges are effective strategies to boost engagement, generate excitement, and reward your community. Here's how to make the most of these activities:

6.3.1 Define Objectives: Determine the purpose and objectives of your contest, giveaway, or challenge. Are you looking to increase brand awareness, gather user-generated content, or reward loyal followers? Clearly defining your objectives helps structure your approach.

6.3.2 Prizes and Incentives: Offer attractive and relevant prizes or incentives that align with your brand and resonate with your audience. The value and desirability of the rewards play a crucial role in motivating participation.

6.3.3 Clear Entry Guidelines: Provide clear and easy-to-follow entry guidelines. Whether it's tagging friends, using specific hashtags, or submitting user-generated content, make the entry process straightforward and accessible to all participants.

6.3.4 Promote and Amplify: Utilize various marketing channels, including your Instagram feed, Stories, website, and email newsletters, to promote your contest, giveaway, or challenge. Leverage influencer collaborations, paid advertising, and cross-promotion with partners to reach a wider audience.

6.3.5 Follow Legal Guidelines: Familiarize yourself with the legal guidelines and regulations regarding contests, giveaways, and challenges in your region. Ensure compliance with all relevant laws to avoid any legal issues.

Hosting contests, giveaways, and challenges not only drive engagement but also create a sense of excitement and anticipation within your community. They provide opportunities to reward and recognize your followers, strengthening their loyalty and connection to your brand.

6.4 Collaborating with Influencers and Partners

Collaborating with influencers and strategic partners can significantly amplify your reach, credibility, and engagement on Instagram. Here's how to establish successful collaborations:

6.4.1 Identify Relevant Influencers: Research and identify influencers whose audience aligns with your target demographic. Look for influencers who have a genuine connection with their followers and whose values align with your brand.

6.4.2 Build Authentic Relationships: Prioritize building authentic relationships with influencers and partners. Engage with their content, provide value, and establish mutual trust and respect. Authenticity is key to successful collaborations.

6.4.3 Define Collaboration Goals: Clearly define the goals and expectations of the collaboration. Whether it's generating brand awareness, creating sponsored content, or hosting joint campaigns, align your objectives with those of your influencers or partners.

6.4.4 Tailor Content to the Audience: Collaborate with influencers and partners to create content that resonates with their audience. Customize the messaging, format, and tone to match their followers' preferences, ensuring a seamless integration of your brand.

6.4.5 Track and Evaluate Performance: Establish metrics to track and evaluate the performance of your collaborations. Monitor engagement levels, follower growth, website traffic, or conversions to assess the impact and return on investment.

Strategic collaborations with influencers and partners can expand your reach, tap into new audiences, and build credibility within your community. By leveraging their influence and expertise, you can strengthen your brand's presence on Instagram.

In Chapter 6, we explored the strategies for building an engaged community on Instagram. By encouraging user engagement and interaction, responding to comments and direct messages, hosting contests, giveaways, and challenges, and collaborating with influencers and partners, you can foster a vibrant and loyal community. Remember, community building is an ongoing process that requires consistent effort and attention. Continuously nurture your community to cultivate strong relationships and create a sense of belonging for your audience.

Chapter 7

Instagram Analytics and Insights

In Chapter 7, we will dive into the world of Instagram analytics and insights. Understanding and leveraging these tools is essential for measuring the performance of your Instagram marketing efforts and optimizing your strategy. This chapter will explore the various analytics features available on Instagram, how to measure and analyze your performance, and how to use insights to optimize your overall marketing strategy.

7.1 Understanding Instagram's Analytics Tools

Instagram provides a range of analytics tools to help you gain valuable insights into your account's performance. These tools offer data and metrics that can guide your decision-making process and help you understand your audience better. Here are some key analytics features on Instagram:

7.1.1 Instagram Insights: Instagram Insights is a built-in analytics tool that provides detailed information about your account's performance. It offers metrics such as impressions, reach, profile views, website clicks, and follower demographics. Insights also provide data on the performance of individual posts and Stories.

7.1.2 Audience Insights: Audience Insights gives you a deeper understanding of your followers. It provides demographic information such as age, gender, location, and language. You can also see when your followers are most active on the platform, allowing you to schedule your content accordingly.

7.1.3 Content Insights: Content Insights provide data on the performance of your individual posts, Stories, and IGTV videos. You can see metrics such as engagement, reach, impressions, and saves. This information helps you identify the types of content that resonate most with your audience.

7.1.4 Activity Insights: Activity Insights provide data on how your audience is interacting with your account. It includes metrics such as profile visits, website clicks, email clicks, and phone call clicks. This data helps you understand how effectively your account is driving actions and conversions.

7.1.5 Hashtag Insights: Hashtag Insights show you how well your hashtags are performing. You can see the reach and engagement generated by each hashtag, allowing you to evaluate the effectiveness of your hashtag strategy.

Understanding these analytics tools is crucial for tracking the performance of your Instagram account and making informed decisions to improve your marketing efforts.

7.2 Measuring and Analyzing Your Performance

To effectively measure and analyze your Instagram performance, you need to track key metrics and derive meaningful insights from the data. Here are some important metrics to consider:

7.2.1 Follower Growth: Monitor your follower growth rate over time. A steady increase indicates that your content is resonating with your target audience and attracting new followers.

7.2.2 Engagement Rate: Engagement rate measures the level of interaction and engagement your content receives. It includes likes, comments, shares, and saves. A high engagement rate indicates that your content is capturing the attention and interest of your audience.

7.2.3 Reach and Impressions: Reach refers to the number of unique accounts that have seen your content, while impressions represent the total number of times your content has been viewed. Tracking reach and impressions helps you understand the visibility and exposure of your content.

7.2.4 Click-Through Rate (CTR): CTR measures the percentage of people who click on a specific link in your bio or in your posts. Monitoring CTR helps you evaluate the effectiveness of your call-to-action and the level of interest in your offerings.

7.2.5 Conversion Rate: If you have a specific conversion goal, such as driving website sign-ups or product purchases, tracking your conversion rate is essential. It measures the percentage of users who complete the desired action.

7.2.6 Audience Demographics: Analyzing your audience demographics, including age, gender, location, and language, helps you understand your target audience better and tailor your content to their preferences.

By regularly measuring and analyzing these metrics, you can gain valuable insights into your performance, identify areas for improvement, and make data-driven decisions to optimize your Instagram marketing strategy.

7.3 Using Insights to Optimize Your Strategy

Instagram insights provide valuable data that can guide your marketing strategy and help you achieve better results. Here's how to leverage insights to optimize your overall approach:

7.3.1 Identify High-Performing Content: Review your content insights to identify the posts, Stories, or IGTV videos that have generated the highest engagement and reach. Analyze the common elements of these top-performing content pieces and replicate their success in future content creation.

7.3.2 Refine Your Posting Schedule: Use audience insights to determine the most active times when your followers are online. Align your posting schedule to these peak times to maximize your content's visibility and engagement potential.

7.3.3 Tailor Your Content Strategy: Analyze audience demographics and preferences to better understand the interests and preferences of your target audience. Use this information to tailor your content strategy, including the topics, formats, and visual styles that resonate most with your followers.

7.3.4 Evaluate Hashtag Performance: Review hashtag insights to identify which hashtags are generating the most reach and engagement. Optimize your hashtag strategy by using relevant and popular hashtags that align with your content and target audience.

7.3.5 Experiment and Test: Instagram insights allow you to track the performance of your experiments and A/B tests. Use this data to evaluate different strategies, such as varying content formats, captions, or call-to-action approaches. Continuously test and iterate to find the most effective tactics for your brand.

7.3.6 Monitor Competitor Performance: Instagram insights also enable you to monitor your competitors' performance. Analyze their content strategy, engagement metrics, and audience demographics to gain insights into their tactics and identify opportunities for differentiation.

By leveraging the insights provided by Instagram analytics tools, you can refine your strategy, optimize your content, and drive better results. Regularly review and analyze the data to stay informed about your audience's preferences and make data-driven decisions.

Chapter 8

Instagram Advertising and Paid Promotions

In Chapter 8, we will explore the world of Instagram advertising and paid promotions. Instagram offers powerful advertising features that allow you to reach a wider audience, increase brand visibility, and drive conversions. This chapter will cover the basics of Instagram ads, setting up effective ad campaigns, targeting specific audiences, and analyzing ad performance and return on investment (ROI).

8.1 Introduction to Instagram Ads

Instagram ads provide a valuable opportunity to showcase your brand, products, or services to a highly engaged audience. Here's an overview of the key features and benefits of Instagram advertising:

8.1.1 Ad Formats: Instagram offers various ad formats, including photo ads, video ads, carousel ads, Stories ads, and IGTV ads. Each format has its own unique features and advantages, allowing you to choose the most suitable format for your marketing goals.

8.1.2 Targeting Options: Instagram ads provide robust targeting options to ensure your ads reach the right audience. You can target based on demographics, interests, behaviors, locations, and even retarget users who have interacted with your brand in the past.

8.1.3 Ad Placements: Instagram ads can appear in different placements, including the Instagram feed, Explore page, Stories, and IGTV. Each placement offers distinct advantages and reaches different segments of the Instagram user base.

8.1.4 Call-to-Action (CTA) Buttons: Instagram ads feature customizable CTA buttons that encourage users to take specific actions, such as "Shop Now," "Learn More," or "Sign Up." These buttons help drive conversions and guide users towards your desired outcomes.

8.1.5 Insights and Performance Tracking: Instagram's analytics tools provide in-depth insights into your ad campaigns' performance. You can track metrics such as impressions, reach, engagement, clicks, and conversions to evaluate the effectiveness of your ads.

8.2 Setting Up Effective Ad Campaigns

To create effective Instagram ad campaigns, it's important to follow a strategic approach. Here are the key steps to setting up successful ad campaigns:

8.2.1 Define Your Objectives: Clearly define your advertising objectives. Are you aiming to increase brand awareness, drive website traffic, generate leads, or boost product sales? Setting specific goals helps you structure your campaigns and measure success.

8.2.2 Understand Your Target Audience: Thoroughly understand your target audience's demographics, interests, and behaviors. This knowledge helps you tailor your ad content and targeting parameters to reach the right audience.

8.2.3 Choose the Right Ad Format: Select the ad format that best suits your campaign objectives and the nature of your content. For example, if you want to showcase multiple products, carousel ads might be more effective than single image ads.

8.2.4 Craft Compelling Ad Creative: Create visually appealing and engaging ad creative that grabs attention and effectively communicates your message. Use high-quality images or videos, compelling captions, and strong visuals to capture the interest of your target audience.

8.2.5 Set Your Budget and Bidding Strategy: Determine your ad campaign budget and select an appropriate bidding strategy. You can choose between automatic bidding, where Instagram optimizes your bids to achieve your objectives, or manual bidding, where you set specific bid amounts.

8.2.6 Define Targeting Parameters: Utilize Instagram's targeting options to reach your desired audience. Narrow down your targeting parameters based on demographics, interests, behaviors, and other relevant factors to maximize the effectiveness of your ads.

8.2.7 Monitor and Optimize: Regularly monitor the performance of your ad campaigns and make necessary optimizations. Adjust your targeting parameters, ad creative, or bidding strategy based on the insights provided by Instagram's analytics tools.

8.3 Targeting Specific Audiences with Ads

Targeting the right audience is crucial for the success of your Instagram ad campaigns. Here are some targeting strategies to help you reach specific audience segments:

8.3.1 Demographic Targeting: Define your audience based on demographics such as age, gender, location, language, and income level. This allows you to tailor your ads to specific groups that are more likely to be interested in your offerings.

8.3.2 Interest-Based Targeting: Target users who have demonstrated interest in specific topics, industries, or products related to your brand. Instagram allows you to target users based on their engagement with related accounts, hashtags, or content.

8.3.3 Behavioral Targeting: Reach users based on their behaviors and actions on Instagram. This includes factors such as past purchases, app usage, website visits, or engagement with specific types of content.

8.3.4 Lookalike Audiences: Create lookalike audiences based on your existing customer base or engaged followers. Instagram's algorithm identifies users who share similar characteristics and interests, expanding your reach to potential customers who are likely to be interested in your brand.

8.4 Analyzing Ad Performance and ROI

To assess the success and return on investment (ROI) of your Instagram ad campaigns, it's crucial to analyze their performance. Here's how you can measure and evaluate your ad performance:

8.4.1 Track Key Metrics: Monitor metrics such as impressions, reach, engagement, clicks, conversions, and cost per result. These metrics provide insights into the effectiveness of your ads and help you understand how they contribute to your marketing objectives.

8.4.2 Conversion Tracking: Set up conversion tracking to measure the specific actions and goals you want users to take, such as purchases,

sign-ups, or downloads. This allows you to calculate the conversion rate and ROI of your ad campaigns accurately.

8.4.3 A/B Testing: Conduct A/B testing to compare the performance of different ad variations. Test different visuals, captions, CTAs, or targeting parameters to identify the most effective elements for your audience.

8.4.4 Optimization Strategies: Continuously optimize your ad campaigns based on the insights you gather. Make adjustments to your targeting, creative, or bidding strategy to improve the performance and ROI of your ads.

8.4.5 ROI Calculation: Calculate the return on investment (ROI) of your Instagram ad campaigns by comparing the revenue generated or the value gained against the cost of running the campaigns. This analysis helps you assess the overall effectiveness of your ad spend.

By leveraging Instagram advertising and paid promotions, you can expand your brand's reach, drive targeted traffic, and achieve your marketing objectives. Regularly analyze the performance of your ads, make data-driven optimizations, and calculate your ROI to ensure the success of your Instagram advertising efforts.

Chapter 9

Leveraging Instagram Shopping and E-commerce

9.1 Setting Up an Instagram Shop

In today's digital age, social media platforms have become an integral part of e-commerce strategies for businesses. Instagram, with its massive user base and visual appeal, offers a unique opportunity for brands to showcase and sell their products directly to their target audience. To take advantage of this, setting up an Instagram Shop is essential. Here are the key steps to get started:

9.1.1 Meet the Eligibility Requirements: Before setting up an Instagram Shop, ensure that you meet the platform's eligibility requirements. You must have a business account, comply with Instagram's merchant agreement and commerce policies, and be located in a supported market.

9.1.2 Connect to a Facebook Page: To create an Instagram Shop, you need to connect it to a Facebook Page. This integration allows you to manage your shop and product catalog seamlessly.

9.1.3 Configure Shop Settings: Customize your Instagram Shop settings, including choosing a shop name, adding a shop description, and selecting a product category. This information helps users understand your brand and the products you offer.

9.1.4 Set Up Payment Methods: Configure your payment methods to enable customers to make purchases directly through Instagram. You can choose from various options, including Instagram Checkout, which provides a streamlined and secure payment process.

9.2 Creating Product Catalogs and Tags

To make your products shoppable on Instagram, you need to create product catalogs and tags. Here's how to do it effectively:

9.2.1 Prepare Your Product Catalog: Organize your products into a structured catalog that includes essential details such as product names, descriptions, prices, and images. You can create catalogs using Facebook Business Manager or an e-commerce platform that integrates with Instagram.

9.2.2 Connect Your Catalog to Instagram: Link your product catalog to your Instagram Shop. This step ensures that your products are available for tagging in your posts and stories.

9.2.3 Add Product Tags: Start tagging your products in your posts and stories. Product tags allow users to tap on the tagged item and view additional information, including the product name, price, and a direct link to purchase.

9.2.4 Utilize Shopping Features: Take advantage of additional shopping features such as product stickers in stories, shopping in Explore, and the Shop tab on your profile. These features provide more opportunities for users to discover and engage with your products.

9.3 Optimizing Shoppable Posts and Stories

Once your Instagram Shop is set up and your products are tagged, it's crucial to optimize your shoppable posts and stories to maximize their impact. Here are some tips to consider

9.3.1 Compelling Visuals: Use high-quality and visually appealing images or videos that showcase your products in the best possible light. Invest in professional photography or create engaging videos to capture the attention of your audience.

9.3.2 Clear Call-to-Action (CTA): Include a clear and compelling call-to-action in your captions or stories, prompting users to tap on the product tag or swipe up to make a purchase. A strong CTA helps drive engagement and conversions.

9.3.3 Contextual Storytelling: Use your posts and stories to tell a story about your products, highlighting their unique features, benefits, or the lifestyle they embody.

Contextual storytelling creates an emotional connection with your audience and enhances the shopping experience.

9.3.4 Promote Limited-time Offers: Leverage the urgency of limited-time offers or exclusive promotions in your shoppable posts and stories. Communicate the scarcity of the offer to drive immediate action from your audience.

9.4 Driving Sales through Instagram

While setting up an Instagram Shop and creating shoppable content are crucial steps, driving sales

requires a comprehensive strategy. Here are some effective tactics to boost your sales on Instagram:

9.4.1 Influencer Collaborations: Collaborate with influencers or micro-influencers in your industry to promote your products. Influencer marketing can help increase brand awareness, credibility, and ultimately drive sales.

9.4.2 User-generated Content (UGC): Encourage your customers to share their experiences with your products by creating user-generated content. UGC not only provides social proof but also helps in building a community of brand advocates who can influence others to make a purchase.

9.4.3 Instagram Ads: Utilize Instagram's advertising platform to reach a broader audience and drive targeted traffic to your shoppable posts and stories. Leverage various ad formats, such as photo ads, video ads, or carousel ads, to showcase your products effectively.

9.4.4 Instagram Insights and Analytics: Regularly analyze your Instagram Insights and use the data to refine your strategy. Monitor key metrics like reach, engagement, and conversion rates to identify trends, understand user behavior, and optimize your content for better results.

9.4.5 Customer Support and Engagement: Provide excellent customer support and engage with your audience promptly. Respond to comments, messages, and inquiries in a timely and helpful manner. Building strong relationships with your customers can foster loyalty and lead to repeat sales.

By leveraging Instagram Shopping and e-commerce effectively businesses can tap into the platform's vast potential for driving sales and reaching new customers. With a well-optimized Instagram Shop, compelling product catalogs, shoppable posts, and a strategic approach, you can create a seamless shopping experience that converts Instagram users into loyal customers.

Chapter 10

Influencer Marketing on Instagram

In today's digital landscape, influencer marketing has emerged as a powerful strategy for brands to connect with their target audience on social media platforms like Instagram. This chapter explores the key aspects of influencer marketing and how businesses can leverage it effectively to drive brand awareness, engagement, and conversions.

10.1 Understanding the Power of Influencer Marketing

Influencer marketing harnesses the influence and reach of popular individuals on social media platforms to promote products or services. Influencers have built a dedicated following and hold sway over their audience's opinions and purchasing decisions. Here's why influencer marketing is powerful:

10.1.1 Authenticity and Trust: Influencers often develop authentic relationships with their followers, who trust their recommendations and perceive them as reliable sources of information.

10.1.2 Targeted Reach: Influencers cater to specific niches or demographics, allowing brands to target their ideal audience effectively. Partnering with influencers ensures that your message reaches the right people.

10.1.3 Creative Content: Influencers are skilled at creating compelling and engaging content that resonates with their followers. Collaborating with influencers can bring fresh and creative perspectives to your brand's marketing efforts.

10.2 Finding and Collaborating with Influencers

Finding the right influencers for your brand requires careful research and consideration. Here are the steps to find and collaborate with influencers:

10.2.1 Define Your Objectives: Determine your goals and what you aim to achieve through influencer marketing. Whether it's increasing brand awareness, driving sales, or expanding your reach, clarifying your objectives will help you identify the most suitable influencers.

10.2.2 Research Relevant Influencers: Conduct thorough research to identify influencers who align with your brand values, target audience, and industry. Explore hashtags, search relevant keywords, and use influencer marketing platforms to find potential collaborators.

10.2.3 Evaluate Influencer Authenticity: Assess an influencer's authenticity by reviewing their content, engagement rates, audience demographics, and comments. Look for genuine engagement, consistent posting, and a loyal follower base.

10.2.4 Establish Communication: Reach out to influencers with a personalized and compelling pitch. Clearly articulate your brand's values, campaign objectives, and the benefits of collaboration. Be open to negotiation and discuss expectations, deliverables, and compensation.

10.3 Negotiating and Measuring Influencer Campaigns

Successful influencer collaborations require effective negotiation and measurement strategies. Here's how to navigate these aspects:

10.3.1 Set Clear Expectations: Clearly define campaign deliverables, content guidelines, and timelines with influencers. Discuss the desired number of posts, specific hashtags, captions, and any disclosure requirements.

10.3.2 Compensation and Contracts: Negotiate compensation based on factors such as the influencer's reach, engagement rates, and the scope of work. Draft a contract that outlines all terms.

10.3.3 Performance Metrics: Establish key performance indicators (KPIs) for your influencer campaigns to track their success. Metrics like reach, engagement, click-through rates, conversions, and return on investment (ROI) can provide valuable insights into the effectiveness of your collaborations.

10.3.4 Influencer Marketing Tools: Utilize influencer marketing platforms and tools to streamline the collaboration process, manage campaigns, and track performance. These tools can help you discover influencers, monitor content, measure results, and simplify payment processes.

10.3.5 FTC Disclosure Guidelines: Familiarize yourself with the Federal Trade Commission (FTC) guidelines regarding disclosure of sponsored content. Ensure that influencers clearly disclose their partnership with your brand to maintain transparency and comply with regulations.

10.4 Authenticity and Disclosure Guidelines

Maintaining authenticity and transparency is crucial for successful influencer marketing. Here's how to ensure authenticity and adhere to disclosure guidelines:

10.4.1 Authentic Brand Alignment: Choose influencers whose values align with your brand. This ensures that the partnership feels natural and authentic to their audience, resulting in higher engagement and trust.

10.4.2 Content Collaboration: Collaborate with influencers on content creation rather than exerting excessive control. Allow influencers to showcase your products or services in a way that resonates with their unique style and storytelling abilities.

10.4.3 Genuine Recommendations: Encourage influencers to provide honest and genuine recommendations to their followers. Authenticity is key to building trust and fostering long-term relationships with both the influencer and their audience.

10.4.4 Clear Disclosure Guidelines: Educate influencers about the FTC's guidelines on disclosing sponsored content. Ensure that they clearly and conspicuously disclose their partnership with your brand in their posts or captions.

10.4.5 Long-term Relationships: Consider building long-term relationships with influencers who consistently deliver results and align with your brand values. Long-term partnerships foster deeper connections, authenticity, and a more genuine representation of your brand.

In conclusion, influencer marketing on Instagram can be a powerful strategy to boost your brand's visibility, reach, and credibility. By understanding the power of influencer marketing, finding the right influencers, negotiating effectively, measuring performance, and maintaining authenticity and transparency, you can create impactful influencer campaigns that drive meaningful results for your business.

Chapter 11

Instagram Strategies for Different Industries

Instagram is a versatile platform that can be leveraged effectively by various industries to achieve their marketing goals. In this chapter, we will explore Instagram strategies for e-commerce brands, service-based businesses, nonprofits and causes, as well as personal brands.

11.1 Instagram Marketing for E-commerce Brands

For e-commerce brands, Instagram offers a powerful platform to showcase products, engage with customers, and drive sales. Here are some strategies to maximize your Instagram presence:

11.1.1 High-Quality Visuals: Invest in visually appealing and high-quality product photography to capture the attention of your audience. Use creative composition, lighting techniques, and editing tools to make your products stand out.

11.1.2 Shoppable Posts and Stories: Take advantage of Instagram's shopping features to create shoppable posts and stories. Tag your products with links to your online store, making it seamless for users to shop directly from your Instagram profile.

11.1.3 User-Generated Content (UGC): Encourage customers to share their experiences with your products by using branded hashtags and running UGC campaigns. Repost UGC on your profile to build social proof and foster a sense of community around your brand.

11.1.4 Influencer Collaborations: Partner with influencers in your niche to promote your products and reach a wider audience. Collaborate on sponsored posts, giveaways, or product reviews to leverage the influencer's credibility and engage with their followers.

11.2 Instagram Strategies for Service-Based Businesses

Service-based businesses can also benefit from an effective Instagram strategy to showcase their expertise, build trust, and attract clients. Consider the following strategies:

11.2.1 Behind-the-Scenes Content: Share behind-the-scenes glimpses of your business to humanize your brand and create a connection with your audience. Show your team, the process of delivering your services, or highlight customer success stories.

11.2.2 Educational Content: Position yourself as an industry expert by sharing educational content, tips, and tutorials related to your services. This helps establish your credibility and attracts potential clients who are looking for valuable insights.

11.2.3 Client Testimonials and Case Studies: Feature testimonials and case studies from satisfied clients to showcase the results and impact of your services. This social proof can help build trust and encourage others to choose your business.

11.2.4 Live Videos and Q&A Sessions: Host live videos to engage with your audience in real-time. Conduct Q&A sessions where you can address common questions, provide valuable insights, and showcase your expertise.

11.3 Instagram Marketing for Nonprofits and Causes

Instagram is a powerful platform for nonprofits and causes to raise awareness, connect with supporters, and drive donations. Consider the following strategies:

11.3.1 Compelling Storytelling: Use Instagram to share impactful stories that highlight the mission and impact of your nonprofit or cause. Use compelling visuals, captions, and videos to engage your audience emotionally and inspire them to take action.

11.3.2 Volunteer Spotlights: Highlight the work of your volunteers and the impact they have on your cause. Feature their stories, achievements, and the difference they make, showcasing the value of volunteering and encouraging others to get involved.

11.3.3 Fundraising Campaigns: Utilize Instagram to promote fundraising campaigns and events. Share updates, progress, and success stories to create a sense of urgency and encourage donations from your followers.

11.3.4 Collaborations and Partnerships: Partner with like-minded influencers, businesses, or other nonprofits to amplify your message and reach a wider audience. Collaborate on campaigns, events, or awareness initiatives to maximize your impact.

11.4 Instagram Best Practices for Personal Brands

For individuals looking to build their personal brand on Instagram, here are some strategies to consider:

11.4.1 Consistent Branding: Develop a consistent visual style, tone, and messaging for your personal brand. This helps create a recognizable and cohesive presence that resonates with your target audience.

11.4.2 Thought Leadership Content: Share valuable insights, tips, and expertise in your niche to establish yourself as a thought leader. Provide unique perspectives, engage in discussions, and showcase your expertise through compelling content.

11.4.3 Authentic Storytelling: Share your personal journey, experiences, and challenges to connect with your audience on a deeper level. Authenticity is key to building trust and fostering a loyal following.

11.4.4 Engaging with Followers: Actively engage with your followers by responding to comments, direct messages, and participating in conversations. Cultivate a community around your personal brand by fostering meaningful interactions and connections.

In conclusion, Instagram strategies vary depending on the industry and goals of the brand. E-commerce brands can focus on visual appeal, shoppable features, and user-generated content. Service-based businesses can showcase expertise, educate their audience, and build trust. Nonprofits and causes can leverage storytelling, collaborations, and fundraising campaigns. Personal brands can establish thought leadership, authenticity, and engage with followers. By understanding the unique needs and opportunities within each industry, businesses and individuals can leverage Instagram to achieve their marketing objectives and connect with their target audience effectively.

Chapter 12

Crisis Management and Reputation Building

In today's digital age, maintaining a positive reputation is essential for businesses and individuals alike. In this chapter, we will explore strategies for effectively managing crises, handling negative feedback, and rebuilding trust to strengthen your brand's reputation.

12.1 Handling Negative Feedback and Public Relations Issues

No brand is immune to negative feedback or public relations issues. It's crucial to have a plan in place to address these situations promptly and effectively. Consider the following strategies:

12.1.1 Listen and Monitor: Regularly monitor social media platforms, review sites, and other online channels to stay informed about any negative feedback or potential issues. Actively listen to your audience's concerns and understand the root causes of their dissatisfaction.

12.1.2 Respond with Empathy: When responding to negative feedback, show empathy and understanding. Acknowledge the issue, apologize if necessary, and assure the person that their concerns are being taken seriously. Avoid getting defensive or engaging in arguments.

12.1.3 Resolve Issues Privately: Whenever possible, try to move the conversation offline and into a private channel. This allows you to address the issue directly and work towards a resolution without further public scrutiny.

12.1.4 Transparency and Honesty: Be transparent and honest in your communications. Clearly explain what steps you are taking to address the issue, and provide updates as the situation progresses. This helps build trust and demonstrates your commitment to resolving the problem.

12.2 Turning Criticism into Opportunities

Negative feedback can be an opportunity for growth and improvement. By adopting a proactive approach, you can turn criticism into positive change. Consider the following strategies:

12.2.1 Active Listening and Learning: Listen attentively to feedback and consider it as a valuable source of insight. Analyze patterns and trends in the feedback to identify areas for improvement and make necessary adjustments to your products, services, or processes.

12.2.2 Engage in Constructive Dialogue: Engage in open and constructive conversations with those providing feedback. Ask clarifying questions, seek to understand their perspective, and explore potential solutions together. This shows that you value their input and are committed to addressing their concerns.

12.2.3 Implementing Feedback: Act upon the feedback received by making tangible changes and improvements. Communicate these changes to your audience, showcasing your responsiveness and commitment to continuous improvement.

12.2.4 Learning from Competitors: Look at how your competitors handle similar criticism or issues. Learn from their successes and failures, adapting strategies that align with your brand values and objectives.

12.3 Rebuilding Trust and Strengthening Your Brand's Reputation

Rebuilding trust after a crisis is essential for restoring your brand's reputation. Consider the following strategies:

12.3.1 Apologize and Take Responsibility: If your brand has made a mistake or been involved in a crisis, take responsibility for the situation. Offer a sincere apology and outline the steps you are taking to rectify the issue and prevent it from happening again.

12.3.2 Consistency and Reliability: Consistently deliver on your brand promises and commitments. Build a reputation for reliability, quality, and excellent customer service. Consistency fosters trust and loyalty among your audience.

12.3.3 Showcase Positive Stories: Share positive stories, testimonials, and success stories that highlight the positive impact of your brand. This helps counterbalance any negative perceptions and rebuild trust in your brand.

12.3.4 Engage in Social Responsibility: Engage in social responsibility initiatives that align with your brand values. Support causes, donate to charities, and communicate your efforts to your audience. This demonstrates your commitment to making a positive impact beyond your business goals.

12.3.5 Influencer Partnerships: Collaborate with influencers or thought leaders who align with your brand values and have a positive reputation. Their endorsement and association can help rebuild trust and enhance your brand's reputation.

In conclusion, effectively managing crises, handling negative feedback, and rebuilding trust are vital for maintaining a strong reputation. By adopting proactive strategies, engaging in constructive dialogue, and demonstrating transparency and accountability, businesses can navigate through challenging situations and emerge stronger. Building a positive reputation takes time and consistent effort, but it is an investment that pays off in the long run, fostering trust, loyalty, and success for your brand.

Chapter 13

Future Trends in Instagram Marketing

As social media platforms continue to evolve, it is crucial for marketers to stay ahead of the curve and adapt their strategies accordingly. In this chapter, we will explore the future trends in Instagram marketing, including the evolving landscape of Instagram features, embracing new formats and technologies, and staying ahead in an ever-changing social media world.

13.1 The Evolving Landscape of Instagram Features

Instagram has continuously introduced new features and updates to enhance user experience and provide new opportunities for marketers. It is important to stay up to date with these changes and leverage them to your advantage. Consider the following trends:

13.1.1 Augmented Reality (AR): Instagram has embraced AR technology with features like filters, effects, and interactive elements. Marketers can leverage AR to create engaging and interactive experiences for their audience, such as virtual try-on for products or immersive branded filters.

13.1.2 Shopping and E-commerce Integration: Instagram has made significant strides in becoming a platform for seamless shopping experiences. Features like Instagram Shopping, product tags, and in-app checkout enable businesses to showcase and sell products directly on the platform. Future trends may include further integration with e-commerce platforms, expanded shopping capabilities, and personalized product recommendations.

13.1.3 Video Content Dominance: Instagram has seen a surge in video content consumption, with features like Instagram Reels and IGTV gaining popularity. Marketers should focus on creating engaging and compelling video content to capture the attention of their audience. Future trends may include more advanced video editing tools, longer video formats, and enhanced discoverability for video content.

13.1.4 Messaging and Direct Communication: Instagram's messaging capabilities, including Direct Messages and Instagram Stories replies, provide opportunities for direct communication and personalized interactions with your audience. Future trends may include improved messaging features, chatbots for customer support, and enhanced ways to connect with followers in real-time.

13.2 Embracing New Formats and Technologies

To stay relevant and capture the attention of your audience, it is important to embrace new formats and technologies that emerge on Instagram. Consider the following trends:

13.2.1 Vertical Content: With the rise of mobile usage, vertical content has become increasingly popular. Marketers should optimize their content for vertical formats, such as Instagram Stories and IGTV, to provide a seamless and immersive viewing experience for their audience.

13.2.2 Short-Form Video: Short-form video content, as seen in Instagram Reels and TikTok, continues to gain traction. Marketers should experiment with creating concise and engaging videos that capture the attention of users in a short span of time.

13.2.3 Interactive and Gamified Content: Interactive content, such as polls, quizzes, and gamified experiences, encourages active participation from users. Marketers should explore ways to incorporate interactive elements into their Instagram content to drive engagement and foster a sense of fun and interactivity.

13.2.4 Influencer Collaborations and Partnerships: Influencer marketing will continue to play a significant role in Instagram marketing. Marketers should stay abreast of emerging influencers and trends, and seek creative ways to collaborate with influencers to reach and engage with their target audience.

13.3 Staying Ahead in an Ever-Changing Social Media World

As the social media landscape evolves, it is crucial for marketers to stay ahead and adapt their strategies to meet the changing needs and preferences of their audience. Consider the following tips:

13.3.1 Stay Updated with Platform Changes: Regularly monitor Instagram updates and announcements to stay informed about new features, algorithm changes, and best practices. Stay connected with industry news and thought leaders to understand emerging trends and opportunities.

13.3.2 Test and Experiment: Don't be afraid to experiment with new features, formats, and strategies. Conduct A/B testing, analyze data, and iterate on your approach to find what works best for your brand and audience.

13.3.3 Focus on Authenticity and Transparency: As social media evolves, users are seeking more authentic and transparent experiences. Build trust with your audience by being genuine, honest, and transparent in your communications and content.

13.3.4 Harness the Power of Data and Analytics: Leverage Instagram's analytics tools and third-party platforms to gain insights into your audience, content performance, and trends. Use this data to refine your strategy, identify opportunities, and make data-driven decisions.

13.3.5 Embrace Cross-Platform Integration: Instagram is just one piece of the social media puzzle. Explore opportunities for cross-platform integration and leverage other social media channels to enhance your overall marketing strategy.

In conclusion, staying ahead in Instagram marketing requires a keen understanding of the evolving landscape, embracing new features and technologies, and constantly adapting to the changing needs of your audience. By staying updated with platform changes, embracing new formats, and focusing on authenticity and transparency, marketers can position themselves for success in an ever-changing social media world.

Chapter 14

Instagram Success Stories and Case Studies

In this chapter, we will delve into inspiring examples of brands that have mastered Instagram marketing, learn from successful influencer campaigns, and analyze different strategies for various goals. By studying these success stories and case studies, you can gain valuable insights and apply them to your own Instagram marketing efforts.

14.1 Inspiring Examples of Brands that Mastered Instagram Marketing

14.1.1 Nike: Nike has been a trailblazer in leveraging Instagram to connect with its audience. They create visually stunning and inspirational content that aligns with their brand values of athleticism, empowerment, and inclusivity. Nike effectively utilizes storytelling to engage their followers, partnering with athletes and influencers to showcase their products in action. They also embrace user-generated content (UGC) by encouraging followers to share their own Nike experiences, fostering a sense of community and loyalty.

14.1.2 Glossier: Glossier has built a cult-like following on Instagram by focusing on minimalism, authenticity, and user engagement. They use Instagram as a platform to share user-generated content, testimonials, and behind-the-scenes glimpses into their brand. Glossier actively listens to their audience and incorporates their feedback into product development and marketing campaigns. Their success lies in creating a community-driven brand that values and empowers its customers.

14.1.3 Airbnb: Airbnb leverages Instagram to showcase unique and beautiful destinations, inspiring wanderlust in their audience. They curate stunning visuals, user-generated content, and travel stories to create an aspirational brand image. Airbnb also utilizes Instagram's features like Instagram Stories and IGTV to provide immersive travel experiences and travel tips. Their Instagram strategy focuses on storytelling, personalization, and fostering a sense of adventure.

14.2 Learning from Successful Influencer Campaigns

Influencer marketing has become a powerful tool for brands to reach and engage with their target audience. Let's explore a few successful influencer campaigns on Instagram:

14.2.1 Daniel Wellington x Influencers: The watch brand Daniel Wellington collaborated with influencers to promote their products. They carefully selected influencers whose style and audience aligned with their brand. The influencers created authentic and visually appealing content showcasing the watches in their everyday lives. This campaign effectively generated brand awareness, increased engagement, and drove sales through influencer endorsements.

14.2.2 Fenty Beauty x Beauty Influencers: Fenty Beauty, founded by Rihanna, partnered with beauty influencers to promote their inclusive range of cosmetics. They collaborated with influencers of diverse backgrounds and skin tones, highlighting the brand's commitment to diversity and representation. The influencers created tutorials, product reviews, and stunning visuals, effectively driving buzz, engagement, and sales for the brand.

14.2.3 GoPro x Adventure Influencers: GoPro, a popular action camera brand, collaborates with adventure influencers to showcase the capabilities of their cameras in extreme sports and outdoor activities. The influencers create thrilling and captivating content that resonates with their adventure-seeking audience. This strategy positions GoPro as a must-have accessory for capturing unforgettable moments and drives interest and demand for their products.

14.3 Analyzing Different Strategies for Various Goals

Different marketing goals require different strategies on Instagram. Let's explore a few scenarios:

14.3.1 Brand Awareness: If your goal is to increase brand awareness, focus on creating visually compelling content that reflects your brand identity. Leverage Instagram's features like Instagram Stories, Reels, and IGTV to tell engaging stories and showcase your products or services. Collaborate with influencers and encourage user-generated content to amplify your reach and connect with new audiences.

14.3.2 Driving Sales: To drive sales, optimize your Instagram profile for shopping by setting up an Instagram Shop and utilizing product tags. Create shoppable posts and stories that provide a seamless purchasing experience for your audience. Offer

 exclusive discounts, promotions, and limited-time offers to incentivize conversions. Track and analyze your sales data to refine your strategy and optimize your conversion funnel.

14.3.3 Building Customer Loyalty: Focus on fostering a sense of community and building customer loyalty by engaging with your audience. Respond to comments and direct messages promptly, and actively participate in conversations. Host contests, giveaways, and challenges to encourage user participation. Show appreciation for your customers by featuring user-generated content and highlighting their stories.

In conclusion, studying Instagram success stories and case studies can provide valuable insights and inspiration for your own marketing efforts. By analyzing successful brands, learning from influencer campaigns, and tailoring strategies to different goals, you can unlock the potential of Instagram as a powerful marketing platform. Remember to stay authentic, engage with your audience, and continuously adapt your approach based on data and insights.

Chapter 15

Conclusion: Your Instagram Marketing Journey Begins!

In this final chapter, we will recap the key takeaways from this book and help you develop an action plan for Instagram success. By reviewing the important concepts and implementing a well-defined strategy, you can embark on your Instagram marketing journey with confidence.

15.1 Recap of Key Takeaways

Throughout this book, we have explored various aspects of Instagram marketing and uncovered strategies and best practices. Let's recap the key takeaways:

- Understanding the Power of Instagram: Instagram is a visual-centric platform that offers immense opportunities for businesses to connect with their target audience and build a strong online presence. It is crucial to recognize the potential and significance of Instagram in the digital age.

- Crafting an Effective Profile: Optimizing your Instagram profile is essential to make a strong first impression. Pay attention to your profile picture, bio, and link to create a compelling and informative profile that resonates with your target audience.

- Planning Engaging Content: Develop a content strategy that aligns with your brand identity and voice. Identify your target audience and create content that appeals to their interests and needs. Plan a mix of static posts, stories, reels, and IGTV videos to keep your content fresh and engaging.

- Harnessing the Power of Hashtags: Hashtags play a crucial role in increasing discoverability and reach on Instagram. Research and utilize relevant hashtags to connect with your target audience. Consider developing branded hashtags to build a community and encourage user-generated content.

- Creating Captivating Visuals: High-quality visuals are the backbone of Instagram marketing. Master composition and lighting techniques to capture stunning photos. Utilize editing apps and filters to enhance your visuals. Incorporate videos and GIFs to diversify your content and increase engagement.

- Building an Engaged Community: Encourage user engagement and interaction by responding to comments and direct messages promptly. Host contests, giveaways, and challenges to foster participation. Collaborate with influencers and partners to expand your reach and credibility.

- Analyzing Performance and Optimizing Strategy: Leverage Instagram's analytics tools to measure and analyze your performance. Use insights to identify trends, understand your audience, and optimize your strategy accordingly. Continuously refine your approach based on data-driven decisions.

15.2 Developing Your Action Plan for Instagram Success

Now that you have a solid understanding of Instagram marketing, it's time to develop your action plan. Here are some steps to guide you:

1. Define Your Goals: Clearly define your marketing goals and objectives. Whether it's increasing brand awareness, driving sales, or building customer loyalty, having specific goals will help you shape your strategy.

2. Identify Your Target Audience: Conduct thorough research to identify your target audience. Understand their demographics, interests, and behaviors to tailor your content and messaging effectively.

3. Craft Your Brand Identity: Develop a strong brand identity and voice that aligns with your target audience. Create a consistent visual aesthetic and storytelling approach that resonates with your followers.

4. Plan Your Content Strategy: Develop a content calendar and plan your content in advance. Consider the types of posts, stories, reels, and IGTV videos you want to create. Align your content with your brand identity and cater to the interests and preferences of your target audience.

5. Utilize Hashtags Strategically: Research and utilize relevant hashtags to increase your reach and discoverability. Experiment with different combinations of hashtags and monitor their performance to identify the most effective ones for your brand.

6. Foster Engagement and Community: Actively engage with your audience by responding to comments, direct messages, and user-generated content. Host contests, giveaways, and challenges to encourage participation. Collaborate with influencers and partners to expand your reach and credibility.

7. Monitor and Analyze Performance: Regularly analyze your performance using Instagram's analytics tools and third-party platforms. Track key

metrics such as reach, engagement, and conversions to evaluate the effectiveness of your strategy. Make data-driven decisions to optimize your approach.

8. Stay Updated with Instagram Trends: Instagram is constantly evolving, introducing new features, formats, and trends. Stay informed about the latest updates and experiment with new strategies to stay ahead of the competitior.

By following these steps and consistently implementing your action plan, you can set yourself up for success on Instagram. Remember that success on Instagram requires dedication, experimentation, and continuous learning.

Congratulations on completing this book and embarking on your Instagram marketing journey! With the knowledge and insights gained, you are well-equipped to navigate the dynamic world of Instagram and achieve your marketing goals. Good luck!

Appendix: Helpful Resources and Tools

In this appendix, we will explore some valuable resources and tools that can assist you in your Instagram marketing efforts. From analytics platforms to content creation tools, these resources can help you analyze your performance, optimize your strategy, and enhance your overall Instagram presence.

Instagram Analytics Tools:

1. Instagram Insights: Instagram provides its own built-in analytics tool called Insights. It offers valuable data on your account's performance, including follower demographics, post reach, engagement metrics, and more. Insights can help you understand your audience better and make data-driven decisions to improve your content strategy.

2. Iconosquare: Iconosquare is a comprehensive Instagram analytics platform that provides in-depth insights and reporting features. It offers data on follower growth, engagement rates, top posts, and competitor analysis. Iconosquare also provides features for scheduling posts and managing comments, making it a versatile tool for managing your Instagram presence.

3. Sprout Social: Sprout Social is a social media management platform that offers robust analytics features. It provides detailed reports on your Instagram

performance, including engagement, reach, and follower demographics. Sprout Social also offers features for scheduling posts, monitoring conversations, and managing multiple social media accounts.

4. Hootsuite: Hootsuite is another popular social media management platform that includes Instagram analytics capabilities. It allows you to track key metrics, monitor hashtags, and measure the success of your Instagram campaigns. Hootsuite also offers features for content scheduling, team collaboration, and social media listening.

5. Later: Later offers a user-friendly Instagram analytics tool that provides data on follower growth, engagement rates, and post performance. It also offers features for scheduling posts, managing content, and optimizing your Instagram strategy.

Content Creation and Editing Tools:

1. Canva: Canva is a versatile graphic design tool that offers a wide range of templates and design elements to create visually appealing Instagram posts. It provides pre-designed templates for various purposes, including quotes, product promotions, and announcements. Canva also allows you to customize designs with your branding elements and offers a user-friendly interface.

2. Adobe Creative Cloud: Adobe Creative Cloud is a suite of creative software that includes Photoshop, Illustrator,

and Premiere Pro. These tools provide advanced editing capabilities, allowing you to create high-quality visuals, edit photos, design graphics, and even create videos for your Instagram content.

3. VSCO: VSCO is a popular photo editing app that offers a wide range of filters and editing tools. It allows you to enhance your photos, adjust colors, and apply artistic effects. VSCO's presets can help you achieve a consistent aesthetic for your Instagram feed.

4. Lightroom: Lightroom is another powerful photo editing app, especially useful for editing and organizing large batches of photos. It provides advanced editing features, presets, and tools for adjusting lighting, colors, and other aspects of your photos. Lightroom also offers sync options, allowing you to edit photos seamlessly across multiple devices.

5. InShot: InShot is a versatile video editing app that offers features such as trimming, cropping, adding music, and applying effects to your videos. It allows you to create engaging and professional-looking video content for your Instagram feed.

Hashtag Research Tools:

1. Hashtagify: Hashtagify is a hashtag research tool that helps you find relevant and popular hashtags for your Instagram posts. It provides insights into hashtag trends,

related hashtags, and hashtag popularity. You can search for specific keywords and explore hashtag suggestions to optimize your hashtag strategy.

2. Display Purposes: Display Purposes is a simple yet effective tool for finding hashtags. It suggests hashtags based on your input and helps you discover relevant options for your content. It also provides filters to exclude specific types of hashtags, ensuring you choose the most suitable ones for your brand.

3. RiteTag: RiteTag offers real-time hashtag suggestions based on their popularity and engagement levels. It provides insights into the performance of hashtags and helps you select the most effective ones for your posts. RiteTag also offers additional features for social media management and analytics.

Competitor Analysis Tools:

1. Social Blade: Social Blade is a platform that offers insights into social media metrics, including follower growth, engagement rates, and historical data. It allows you to track your own performance and compare it to your competitors. Social Blade also provides rankings and statistics for top Instagram accounts in various niches.

2. Sprout Social's Competitor Analysis: If you're using Sprout Social for your Instagram management, you can leverage its competitor analysis features. It allows you to monitor your competitors' performance, benchmark your

metrics against theirs, and identify areas for improvement. This can provide valuable insights and inspiration for your own Instagram strategy.

Influencer Discovery Platforms:

Collaborating with influencers can significantly amplify your Instagram marketing efforts. Influencer discovery platforms can help you find influencers who align with your brand and target audience. Here are a few platforms to consider:

- Upfluence: Upfluence is an influencer marketing platform that allows you to discover influencers, analyze their audience demographics, and manage influencer campaigns

. It provides valuable insights and analytics to help you make informed decisions.

- HYPR: HYPR is an influencer discovery and analytics platform that offers a vast database of influencers. It allows you to search for influencers based on specific criteria, such as location, interests, and engagement rates. HYPR also provides detailed analytics to evaluate the performance of influencers.

- Traackr: Traackr is an influencer marketing platform that helps you identify and connect with relevant influencers. It offers advanced search capabilities, influencer relationship management features, and analytics to measure the impact of your influencer campaigns.

Instagram Scheduling and Management Tools:

To maintain a consistent posting schedule and efficiently manage your Instagram presence, scheduling and management tools can be immensely helpful. These tools enable you to plan and schedule your content in advance, track engagement, and streamline your workflow. Here are a few popular options:

- Later: Later offers a comprehensive Instagram scheduling and management platform. It allows you to visually plan your Instagram feed, schedule posts, and automatically publish them at the desired times. Later also provides content analytics and social media management features.

- Buffer: Buffer is a social media management platform that includes Instagram scheduling capabilities. It enables you to plan and schedule your Instagram posts, collaborate with team members, and track post performance. Buffer also offers integration with other social media platforms for cross-channel scheduling.

- Hootsuite: Hootsuite is a widely used social media management tool that supports Instagram scheduling. It allows you to schedule and publish your Instagram content, monitor comments and mentions, and analyze performance metrics. Hootsuite also offers features for team collaboration and content curation.

These are just a few examples of the many resources and tools available to support your Instagram marketing efforts. Depending on your specific needs and goals, you can explore and leverage these tools to enhance your analytics, content creation, hashtag strategy, and competitor analysis. Remember to choose tools that align with your requirements and budget.

By utilizing these resources effectively, you can gain a deeper understanding of your Instagram performance, optimize your strategy, and stay ahead in the competitive social media landscape.

Note: The landscape of social media tools and platforms is constantly evolving. Stay updated on new releases and advancements in the industry to make the most out of the available resources and tools.

www.ingramcontent.com/pod-product-compliance
Lightning Source LLC
Chambersburg PA
CBHW020448220526
45464CB00002B/911